Looking on the **BRIGHT SIDE** with Elmo

A Book about Positivity

Jill Colella

Lerner Publications ◆ Minneapolis

Sesame Street's mission has always been about teaching kids much more than simply the ABCs and 123s. This series of books about nurturing the positive character traits of generosity, respect, empathy, positive thinking, resilience, and persistence will help children grow into the best versions of themselves. So come along with your funny, furry friends from Sesame Street as they learn about making themselves—and the world—smarter, stronger, and kinder.

—Sincerely, the Editors at Sesame Street

TABLE OF CONTENTS

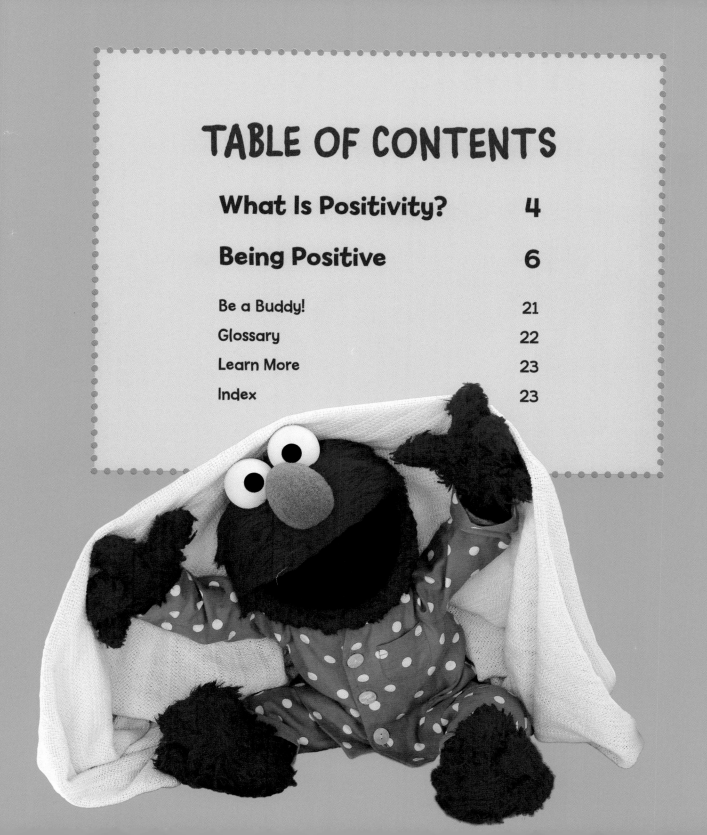

What Is Positivity?

Elmo likes to think about happy things.

Positivity means seeing the good parts in any situation.

Being Positive

When we face challenges, looking on the bright side helps us keep going.

When I have the sniffles, I get to stay inside and color.

No one is positive all the time.

Feelings such as
happiness and
sadness come and go.

Can you think of a time when you did not feel positive?

Rainy days can be frustrating
or disappointing.

And there is a chance of a rainbow!

But they also help the flowers grow.

Doing or noticing little things
can make us feel happy.

Wearing my tutu makes me feel happy.

When we are stuck, we
can look for solutions.

I didn't believe that I could tie my shoes until Grover told me to keep trying.

We can ask for help.

Think about the great things you've already learned and done.

What was something you did that you were proud of?

And more good things are on their way!

People who are hopeful are called optimists.

We cannot always know what problems will pop up. But seeing the bright side helps us move forward.

BE A BUDDY!

Keep a "good things" journal. Each day draw a picture of something good that happened or a happy thought you had. Keep your drawings, and look through them. These memories will help you feel positive.

Glossary

happy: feeling joy

optimist: a person who is hopeful

positivity: being hopeful

solution: an idea to solve a problem

Learn More

Bullis, Amber. *Feeling Happy.*
Minneapolis: Jump!, 2020.

Colella, Jill. *Bouncing Back with Big Bird:
A Book about Resilience.* Minneapolis: Lerner
Publications, 2021.

Lang, Sheri. *My Thoughts and Feelings: What Are You
Feeling?* New York: Rosen, 2020.

Index

Photo Acknowledgments

Additional image credits: Sun_Shine/Shutterstock.com, p. 4; Rawpixel.com/Shutterstock.com, pp. 5, 6; 21MARCH/Shutterstock.com, p. 7; fizkes/Shutterstock.com, p. 8; Pressmaster/Shutterstock.com, p. 9; A3pfamily/Shutterstock.com, p. 10; perfectlab/Shutterstock.com, p. 11; Africa Studio/Shutterstock.com, p. 12; Monkey Business Images/Shutterstock.com, p. 13; Phil's Mommy/Shutterstock.com, p. 14; Lorena Fernandez/Shutterstock.com, p. 15; Pixel-Shot/Shutterstock.com, p. 16; Fotokostic/Shutterstock.com, p. 17; ESB Professional/Shutterstock.com, p. 18; Olesia Bilkei/Shutterstock.com, p. 19; iofoto/Shutterstock.com, p. 20.

For the girls: LKAT, PKAT, and EVAF

Lerner Publications Company
An imprint of Lerner Publishing Group, Inc.
241 First Avenue North
Minneapolis, MN 55401 USA

For reading levels and more information, look up this title at www.lernerbooks.com.

Main body text set in Billy Infant. Typeface provided by SparkyType.

Editor: Rebecca Higgins **Photo Editor:** Brianna Kaiser

Library of Congress Cataloging-in-Publication Data

Names: Colella, Jill, author.
Title: Looking on the bright side with Elmo : a book about positivity / Jill Colella.
Description: Minneapolis : Lerner Publications, [2021] | Series: Sesame Street character guides | Includes bibliographical references and index. | Audience: Ages 4-8 | Audience: Grades K-1 | Summary: "Elmo and friends learn about positivity and how thoughts impact us. Kids will discover that all feelings are valid, what it means to be an optimist, and how to look on the bright side"—Provided by publisher.
Identifiers: LCCN 2020009470 (print) | LCCN 2020009471 (ebook) | ISBN 9781728403892 (library binding) | ISBN 9781728418735 (ebook)
Subjects: LCSH: Optimism in children—Juvenile literature. | Optimism—Juvenile literature.
Classification: LCC BF723.O67 C645 2021 (print) | LCC BF723.O67 (ebook) | DDC 155.4/19—dc23

LC record available at https://lccn.loc.gov/2020009470
LC ebook record available at https://lccn.loc.gov/2020009471

Manufactured in the United States of America
1-48389-48903-6/4/2020